Smithsonian

Ultimate Predators

Silver Dolphin

Silver Dolphin Books
An imprint of Printers Row Publishing Group
A division of Readerlink Distribution Services, LLC
10350 Barnes Canyon Road, Suite 100, San Diego, CA 92121
www.silverdolphinbooks.com

ISBN 978-1-62686-761-1
Manufactured, printed, and assembled in the Stevens Point, Wisconsin, U.S.A.
Sixth printing, April 2019. WOR/04/19
23 22 21 20 19   6 7 8 9 10

The Age of Dinosaurs written by Megan Roth
Reptiles written by Brenda Scott Royce
Sharks written by Brenda Scott Royce
Big Cats and Other Predators written by Brenda Scott Royce
Book designed by Kat Godard

The Age of Dinosaurs reviewed by Mike Brett-Surman, PhD, Museum Specialist for Fossil
Dinosaurs, Reptiles, Amphibians, and Fish, National Museum of Natural History, Smithsonian.

Reptiles, Sharks, and *Big Cats and Other Predators* reviewed by Dr. Don E. Wilson, Curator Emeritus
of the Department of Vertebrate Zoology, National Museum of Natural History, Smithsonian.

For Smithsonian Enterprises:
Kealy Gordon, Product Development Manager, Licensing
Ellen Nanney, Licensing Manager
Brigid Ferraro, Vice President, Education and Consumer Products
Carol LeBlanc, Senior Vice President, Education and Consumer Products

Image Credits:
Cover: Images © Thinkstock
Back cover: Images © Thinkstock
Front matter: Images © Thinkstock
The Age of Dinosaurs: Images © SuperStock, Inc., Thinkstock, Smithsonian Institution,
Silver Dolphin Books
Reptiles: Images © Thinkstock
Sharks: Images © Superstock, Inc., Thinkstock, Gyik Toma, NORFANZ Founding Parties
Big Cats and Other Predators: Images © SuperStock, Inc., Thinkstock

Every effort has been made to contact copyright holders for the images in this book. If you are
the copyright holder of any uncredited image herein, please contact us at Silver Dolphin Books,
10350 Barnes Canyon Road, Suite 100, San Diego, CA 92121.

CONTENTS

A NOTE TO PARENTS AND TEACHERS

Smithsonian Readers were created for children who are just starting on the amazing road to reading. These engaging books support the acquisition of reading skills, encourage children to learn about the world around them, and help to foster a lifelong love of books. These high-interest informational texts contain fascinating, real-world content designed to appeal to beginning readers. This early access to high-quality books provides an essential reading foundation that students will rely on throughout their school career.

The five levels in the Smithsonian Readers series target different stages of learning abilities. Each child is unique; age or grade level does not determine a particular reading level.

When sharing a book with beginning readers, read in short stretches, pausing often to talk about the pictures. Have younger children turn the pages and point to the pictures and familiar words. And be sure to reread favorite parts. As children become more independent readers, encourage them to share the ideas they are reading about and to discuss ideas and questions they have. Learning practice can be further extended with the quizzes after each title.

There is no right or wrong way to share books with children. You are setting a pattern of enjoying and exploring books that will set a literacy foundation for their entire school career. Find time to read with your child, and pass on the amazing world of literacy.

Adria F. Klein, Ph.D.
Professor Emeritus
California State University San Bernardino

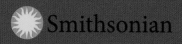
The Age of Dinosaurs

Megan Roth

Contents

Dinosaurs

Dinosaurs are a diverse and fascinating group of animals!

In 1842, a scientist named Richard Owen wanted to give a name to the animals whose huge fossilized bones people were finding. He used the Greek word *deinos*, which means "fearfully great," and *saur*, which means "lizard," so *dinosaur* means "fearfully great lizard." But not all dinosaurs should be feared—and dinosaurs were not true lizards!

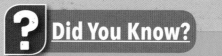 **Did You Know?**

Dinosaurs are part of the **archosaur** group, which includes pterosaurs, crocodiles, and birds!

The Age of Dinosaurs

Dinosaurs first appeared on Earth over 250 million years ago!

They lived during the Mesozoic era, which is divided into three periods. The Triassic period was 252–201 million years ago. The Jurassic period was 201–145 million years ago. The Cretaceous period was 145–66 million years ago.

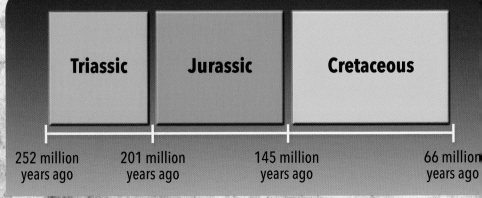

Triassic	Jurassic	Cretaceous
252 million years ago	201 million years ago	145 million years ago	66 million years ago

Some dinosaur groups lived during all three periods. Others were around during just one or two.

Dinosaurs weren't the only **prehistoric** creatures. They weren't even the first creatures. Life began over 3.6 billion years ago in the oceans and eventually made its way onto land. Plants, bugs, and reptiles were already on Earth by the time dinosaurs arrived.

What Is a Fossil?

Fossils are evidence of life from the geologic past.

If a living thing, like a dinosaur, dies, and happens to be buried in a way that keeps air, scavengers, and bacteria from getting to it, it can become a fossil. Over time, the soft parts of the dinosaur **decay** and minerals in the groundwater are added to the actual animal remains and then harden into rock.

Minerals from the earth can soak into the animal's skeleton and sometimes preserve whole animals in rock. Dinosaur fossils have been found on every continent, even Antarctica.

Without fossils, we wouldn't know anything about dinosaurs. Even with fossils, much of what we now know about dinosaurs comes from educated hypotheses and scientific research.

Scientists look at where a fossil was found and what other fossils were surrounding it. **Paleontologists** study fossils, but most fossils are found by ordinary people.

 **Did You Know?**

The fossil of a hadrosaur that lived 67 million years ago was found in North Dakota by 16-year-old Tyler Lyson.

Ancient people all around the world found dinosaur fossils, but they had no idea what they were. They made up stories, myths, and legends about these monsters.

Even when the first recorded dinosaur fossil, which was a Megalosaurus, was described in 1824, people didn't know that these ancient animals were dinosaurs. The word *dinosaur* wasn't even used until 1842.

Figuring out the mystery of dinosaurs is difficult. Even after scientists knew about dinosaurs, they'd get things wrong.

In 1877, paleontologist O.C. Marsh discovered a dinosaur and named it Apatosaurus. In 1879, he came across another fossil, which he named Brontosaurus. Then in 1903, paleontologist Elmer Riggs noticed that the two looked nearly identical and determined they were the same type of dinosaur—Apatosaurus.

Dinosaur Colors & Feathers

Scientists are able to build a dinosaur skeleton based on the information they get from its fossils. They can tell what the dinosaur's scales were like and if it had feathers. But how do they know what color the dinosaur was?

Scientists found that dinosaur feathers have melanosome sacs within their cells.

These sacs are filled with pigments, or colors, that are shaped and arranged differently depending on the color of the dinosaur.

Sinosauropteryx was the first feathered dinosaur to be scientifically named. Scientists studied a piece of its tail to determine it was striped orange and white. No one knows exactly what color the rest of the dinosaur was.

Some scientists think the changes melanin goes through over millions of years of fossilization make information about a dinosaur's color inaccurate. So the research continues!

All in the Hips

Hundreds of different kinds of dinosaurs lived on Earth millions of years ago. Paleontologists have discovered more than 1,200 types of dinosaurs.

These types are put into individual **species**. Then, scientists sort them into two different major groups: Saurischia and Ornithischia. Each group shares special features of bone and muscle.

lizard hips

Dinosaurs in the Saurischia group are nicknamed "lizard hips." They had hips like a lizard's, with one of the bones pointing forward.

The Saurischia group includes theropods, like Tyrannosaurus rex, and sauropods, like Brachiosaurus.

Those in the Ornithischia group are nicknamed "bird hips." They had hips like a bird's, with all the lower hipbones pointing backward, and they ate plants.

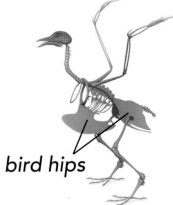

bird hips

The Ornithischia group is made up of ornithopods, stegosaurs, pachycephalosaurs, ankylosaurs, and ceratopsians.

Stegosaurs

Stegosaurs lived in the Jurassic and the first third of the Cretaceous period, walking on all four, and eating low-growing plants.

Stegosaurs were not the biggest dinosaurs, but they looked threatening because of the two rows of bony plates down their backs and spikes at the end of their tails.

The most recognizable stegosaur is Stegosaurus.

Stegosaurus was as big as two rhinoceroses and had tough skin; a heavy, spiked tail; and a brain the size of a golf ball. It would have been a prime target for the hungry meat-eaters of the day.

The line of bony plates that stood up along Stegosaurus's back may have helped it control its temperature. At first, people thought these plates lay flat, like roof tiles, which is how the dinosaur got its name, which means "roofed lizard."

Ankylosaurus

Ankylosaurs were slow-moving plant-eaters. They developed elaborate armor as a defense against meat-eating dinosaurs.

Ankylosaurs have been called "walking tanks." The top of the body was covered in hard, bony plates reinforced by lumps and spikes that protected against predators—especially Tyrannosaurus rex.

Even the hungriest meat-eater of the Mesozoic era would find ankylosaurs hard to swallow.

As long as it stayed flat against the ground and didn't let a predator get to its soft underbelly, this dinosaur would be safe in an attack. Ankylosaurs were some of the last dinosaurs to die out at the end of the Cretaceous period.

? Did You Know?

Ankylosaurs' teeth were shaped like broad leaves.

Triceratops

Triceratops is one of the most recognized Ceratopsian dinosaurs. It was the biggest of the horned dinosaurs, and was one of the last dinosaurs to become **extinct**.

Ceratopsians lived during the Cretaceous period. They had beaks and teeth in their cheeks to grind up the leaves and plants that they ate. Ceratopsians are called "horned dinosaurs" because many had horns and **frills**.

Triceratops was a plant-eater and used its strong, sharp beak to help it bite through thick branches and stems.

Triceratops developed tough skin and horns for protection against meat-eating dinosaurs.

Triceratops had three sharp horns on its head to defend itself, and a big frill on its neck that made Triceratops look bigger than it really was. The frill also may have kept attackers from reaching behind its head to get at its body.

Tyrannosaurus rex

The huge Tyrannosaurus rex had a powerful bite and sharp teeth. Many consider T. rex to be one scary dinosaur. It was a fierce hunter, but also searched for dead animals.

Tyrannosaurus rex's arms were strangely small, but they were a lot stronger than they look.

? Did You Know?

T. rex's arms were too small to reach its mouth, but they were extremely powerful.

Surprisingly, Tyrannosaurus rex hatchlings may have been covered in feathers. There is still a lot to learn about this fierce predator.

We do know that they had sharp teeth, up to 12 inches long, that were ridged to tear through meat.

T. rex's long and thick tail balanced out its enormous body and helped it move quickly.

Velociraptor

Velociraptor was a fierce and fast-moving meat-eater about the size of a turkey. It was an aggressive hunter; had needle-sharp teeth; a long, pointed jaw; and sharp claws on its hands. Its four-inch-long retractable claws were used to attack prey.

This feathered hunter had excellent vision. The bones near its eyes suggest it may have hunted at night.

  **Did You Know?**

Standing upright on two legs, Velociraptor could run up to 20 miles per hour.

Velociraptor's stiff tail could not bend, so it was probably used for balance. It was covered in feathers, but could not fly.

Small forearms made it impossible for Velociraptor to fly, even though it shares many characteristics with modern birds.

Avimimus was a small meat-eating dinosaur that lived in the late Cretaceous period. With its long neck and legs, it looked a bit like a miniature ostrich but, like Velociraptor, was only about the size of a turkey.

Instead of a tooth-filled jaw, it had a strong, parrotlike beak. A toothless beak means it probably ate nuts, fruit, and small animals.

This birdlike dinosaur had long, slender legs that helped it chase prey quickly.

Avimimus had a large brain for its body size.

Avimimus had short arms that were able to fold like modern birds' wings. Each arm had three sharp claws on the end.

Sauropods started out in the late Triassic period as plant-eaters that walked on two legs and were rather small. But by the beginning of the Jurassic period, this group of dinosaurs **evolved** and started walking on all four legs. They grew to be some of the biggest and most recognizable dinosaurs.

Sauropods' small heads kept their long necks light enough to reach food high in the trees.

Brachiosaurus was one of the biggest sauropod dinosaurs, reaching about 60 feet tall, spanning 85 feet from nose to tail, and weighing up to 50 tons.

When the first Brachiosaurus fossils were found, people thought the animals would have been too heavy to live on land. Some thought that they actually lived in water, holding only their heads up above the surface, but this was later shown to be false.

 **Did You Know?**

Brachiosaurus could eat up to 500 pounds of plant food every day.

Extinction

Dinosaurs stomped around on Earth for 165 million years. But today they are extinct, though modern birds are considered to be the descendents of dinosaurs.

So what happened? How did these powerful and varied creatures get wiped off the Earth?

Some people think the Earth's climate changed toward the end of the Cretaceous period, becoming too cold for dinosaurs to survive.

Others think that clouds of ash from erupting volcanoes blocked the sun. With no sunlight, plants died, plant-eating animals starved, and then the meat-eaters had no food either.

Still others think a giant **asteroid** struck the Earth, spewing dust into the air and blocking out the sun. Scientists have found an underwater crater near Mexico that may be the asteroid's impact site.

Did You Know?

The dinosaurs weren't the only casualties of this mass extinction. Flying reptiles like pterosaurs, some ocean life, and many of the insect and plant species on land got wiped out.

Most paleontologists believe that a combination of the asteroid impact, with extensive volcanism, caused the mass extinction. Thankfully, we keep finding fossils, so there is still much to be learned and discovered!

Dinosaurs Quiz

1. What does the Greek word *saur* mean?
   a. Great
   b. Feared
   c. Lizard
   d. Reptile

2. What year did the word *dinosaur* start being used by scientists?
   a. 1824
   b. 1842
   c. 1912
   d. 1756

3. Which animals are relatives of dinosaurs?
   a. Mammals
   b. Snakes
   c. Birds
   d. Rhinoceroses

4. What is the name for a scientist who studies fossils?
   a. Pathologist
   b. Herbivore
   c. Paleontologist
   d. Carnivore

5. Which dinosaur was not a plant-eater?
    a. Tyrannosaurus rex
    b. Brachiosaurus
    c. Triceratops
    d. Ankylosaurus

6. What were lizard-hipped dinosaurs called?
    a. Saurischians
    b. Ornithischians
    c. Pachycephalosaurs
    d. Ceratopsians

7. Which dinosaur name means "roofed lizard"?
    a. Triceratops
    b. Stegosaurus
    c. Brachiosaurus
    d. Ankylosaurus

8. Which fully grown dinosaur is the size of a turkey?
    a. Brachiosaurus
    b. Triceratops
    c. Stegosaurus
    d. Avimimus

Answers: 1) c 2) b 3) c 4) c 5) a 6) a 7) b 8) d

Glossary

Archosaur the group of reptiles—including pseudosuchians, dinosaurs, crocodiles, and pterosaurs—that ruled the land during the Mesozoic era

Asteroid a rock in space; it can be as small as a boulder or as big as a country

Decay to be slowly destroyed or broken down by natural processes

Evolved changed very slowly to become something new

Extinct a species that is no longer living

Fossils the remains of prehistoric life found in stone, or evidence of life from the geologic past

Frills sheets or plates of skull bones on the heads of horned dinosaurs

Paleontologists scientists who study fossils

Prehistoric the time before people began recording history

Species a group of living things different from all other groups

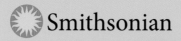
Reptiles

Brenda Scott Royce

Contents

What Is a Reptile?

Reptiles are **cold-blooded** creatures with rough, scaly skin. They are **vertebrates**, which means they have a backbone or spine. Snakes, turtles, lizards, and alligators are all types of reptiles.

There are more than ten thousand known types of reptiles in the world. Scientists discover new reptile **species** each year. These fascinating creatures have roamed the Earth for about 315 million years!

Really Cool Reptiles

The Galapagos tortoise is the world's largest tortoise. This giant tortoise weighs more than a full-grown gorilla!

The male Jackson's chameleon has three horns on its head. Its horns make it look like a tiny Triceratops! Males use their horns to defend their space. Females do not have horns.

The blue-tongued skink is named for the color of its tongue. When frightened, the skink sticks its tongue out at attackers.

Lizards cannot fly, but the Draco lizard comes close. The Draco lizard has flaps of skin on both sides of its body. It spreads these flaps and glides on the wind! This amazing ability helps the lizard flee from predators and find meals.

Reptile Homes

Reptiles live on every continent except Antarctica.

Different reptiles live in different types of habitats. Each species has **adaptations**, or special characteristics, that help it thrive in its environment.

Some reptiles are right at home in the hot, dry desert. Desert tortoises can survive for a year without drinking any water. They get most of their water from the foods they eat.

Other reptiles hang out in the jungle. The green tree python loops its body over a tree branch like a coiled rope. It grasps the branch with its tail when striking out at passing prey.

Reptiles can be found in lakes, rivers, and oceans. Crocodiles and alligators spend most of their time in the water.

What's for Dinner?

Most reptiles are predators; they eat other animals for food. Small reptiles eat insects. A chameleon catches a cricket with its long, sticky tongue.

? DID YOU KNOW? A chameleon's tongue can accelerate five times faster than a fighter jet!

Some reptiles are **herbivores**. Desert tortoises eat grass, plants, and flowers. The green iguana mostly eats leaves but also enjoys fruit.

Snakes are **carnivores**. They eat other animals. Snakes' favorite foods include rodents, birds, eggs, and frogs.

Some snakes have deep pits around their mouths that help them detect heat. The ability to sense heat helps snakes hunt at night.

Shells and Scales

Reptiles may be smooth, rough, or bumpy. Despite what many people think, reptiles are not slimy.

Snake skin is made up of scales. Scales come in different shapes and colors. Most overlap like tiles on the roof of a house. Snake scales are made of **keratin**, the same protein found in human fingernails!

As they grow, reptiles replace the outer layer of their skin. A snake sheds all its skin at once, leaving behind one long piece.

Turtles and tortoises have hard shells. Shells vary in shape, size, and color depending on the species. The star tortoise has star-shaped markings on its shell.

Keeping Warm

Reptiles don't have fur or feathers to keep them warm. Reptiles are cold-blooded creatures. They do not produce their own body heat. Instead they depend on outside sources, such as the sun.

Reptiles take on the temperature of their surroundings. A lizard basks in the sun to warm up. When it gets too hot, the lizard will move to a shady spot.

Some lizards change the shade of their skin based on temperature. In the morning, their skin is dark. Dark colors absorb more heat. By midday, they've soaked up plenty of heat from the sun, and their skin tone lightens.

Hide and Seek

Some reptiles are known for their **camouflage**. Their colors and patterns blend with rocks, branches, or trees. The leaf gecko is a master of disguise. Its body looks like a leaf.

Chameleons can change color to match their surroundings. Camouflage helps animals hide from potential predators.

Tiny crystals located under the chameleon's skin are what enable it to change color. As the crystals contract and expand, they reflect different wavelengths of light.

Some reptiles use camouflage to get close to prey without being seen. The patterns on the Gaboon viper's back help it blend in with leaves on the forest floor. Once hidden, the viper waits patiently for a rodent or bird to approach. Then it strikes suddenly!

DID YOU KNOW? The Gaboon viper has the longest fangs of any snake.

Stay Away!

In the animal kingdom, bright colors are often a sign of danger. They signify that an animal is poisonous or **venomous**.

The coral snake's bright colors warn others to stay away. This snake has a dangerous bite!

A cobra can spread out its neck to make itself appear bigger and more threatening.

The rattlesnake has a built-in alarm. When it feels threatened, a rattlesnake wriggles the rattle at the end of its tail.

DID YOU KNOW?

Each time a rattlesnake sheds its skin, its rattle gains another segment. That's why older rattlesnakes usually have longer rattles than young snakes.

When a frilled lizard feels threatened, it puts on a dazzling display! Flaps of skin around its head pop out like an expanded umbrella. It stands upright and hisses at its would-be attacker.

Turtles and Tortoises

What's the difference between a turtle and a tortoise?

A tortoise is a type of turtle. Turtles are usually found near water, while tortoises live on land.

Turtles and tortoises have hard shells for protection. Few predators can break through an adult turtle's shell.

A turtle cannot crawl out of its shell; it is permanently attached.

The world's largest turtle makes its home in the ocean. The leatherback sea turtle weighs up to 2,000 pounds! Its powerful flippers propel it through the water with ease. This giant predator primarily eats jellyfish.

Turtles don't have teeth! They bite their food with a sharp upper beak.

Snakes

Some snakes kill their prey by squeezing it. These snakes are known as **constrictors**. Boas and pythons are constrictors. Each time its victim exhales, the snake tightens its coils. Eventually the prey's heart stops, and the snake eats it whole.

Other snakes kill their prey by biting it. A rattlesnake uses hollow fangs to inject venom into its prey. Some types of venom work instantly, killing prey within seconds. Others act slowly, weakening prey so that it is easier to catch.

A rattlesnake's fangs stay hidden inside a layer of skin until it is ready to strike.

Lizards

There are more than 6,000 types of lizards. Iguanas, chameleons, and geckos are all lizards.

A dwarf gecko can curl up on a dime. A green iguana can be 6 feet long!

The gecko's toes are great at gripping! Tiny hairs on the gecko's toe pads help it climb up smooth surfaces.

This colorful creature is a collared lizard. The black stripes around its neck look like a shirt collar.

When in danger, some lizards shed, or "drop," their tails. The twitching tail distracts a hungry predator, and the lucky lizard escapes. The lizard will eventually regrow its missing tail.

Dragons

These are not fairy-tale dragons. They cannot fly, and they don't breathe fire. These dragons belong to the lizard family.

The Komodo dragon is the world's largest lizard, averaging 10 feet long when grown. Large, sawlike teeth and a venomous bite make these dragons powerful predators. They eat a wide range of animals, from rodents to water buffalo.

DID YOU KNOW? *Varanus bitatawa*, a relative of the Komodo dragon, was discovered in 2009. This secretive species spends its time high up in the trees.

The bearded dragon has spiky scales on its throat. It inflates its "beard" like a balloon to frighten enemies.

The Chinese water dragon is an excellent climber and a strong swimmer. When startled, it dives into the water for safety. It can remain underwater for 20 minutes without coming up for air!

Alligators & Crocodiles

What's the difference?

Alligators have short, wide heads in the shape of a U.

Crocodile heads are long and pointed like the letter V.

Alligators are found in freshwater rivers, swamps, and lakes.

Crocodiles have special glands that allow them to tolerate salt water. They can be found in fresh or saltwater habitats.

Both alligators and crocodiles are at home in the water. On land, these great reptiles can run fast—but only in short bursts.

The gharial is related to crocodiles and alligators. It has a long, skinny snout and more than 100 teeth. Its needle-sharp teeth help the gharial catch its favorite meal—fish!

DID YOU KNOW? When a crocodile or alligator loses a tooth, a new one grows in its place. Over its lifetime, this gharial could replace its teeth dozens of times.

At up to 20 feet long, the saltwater crocodile is the world's biggest reptile. A "saltie" can leap high to grab an animal near the water's edge.

Baby Reptiles

Sea turtle mothers bury their eggs on the beach. When the eggs hatch, the baby turtles race to the sea. This journey can be very dangerous for the **hatchlings**. There are plenty of predators on the seashore. Once the baby turtles reach the water they begin what is called a "swimming frenzy."

A sea turtle may lay up to 100 eggs at one time. That's a lot of brothers and sisters!

Most reptiles abandon their eggs, but crocodile moms stick around to guard them.

A crocodile mother carries a baby in her mouth to keep him safe.

Sometimes, the baby rides on her back. The mother will remain close to her babies for several months.

Reptiles Quiz

1. Which continent is NOT home to any reptiles?
   a. Asia
   b. Antarctica
   c. Australia
   d. Africa

2. What do herbivores eat?
   a. Plants
   b. Rodents
   c. Frogs
   d. Eggs

3. Which snake has the longest fangs?
   a. Western diamondback rattlesnake
   b. Gaboon viper
   c. King cobra
   d. Copperhead

4. About how much does a leatherback sea turtle weigh?
   a. 100 pounds
   b. 2,000 pounds
   c. 20 pounds
   d. 900 pounds

5. Which is NOT a type of lizard?
   a. Iguana
   b. Chameleon
   c. Gecko
   d. Python

6. What reptile has special glands that allow it to live in salt water?
   a. Boa constrictor
   b. Rattlesnake
   c. Alligator
   d. Crocodile

7. Which is the largest reptile?
   a. Saltwater crocodile
   b. American alligator
   c. Aldabra tortoise
   d. Dwarf gecko

8. How many eggs can a sea turtle lay at one time?
   a. 1
   b. 100
   c. 1,000
   d. 10,000

Glossary

Adaptations special characteristics that help an animal survive in its environment

Camouflage an animal's colors or markings that help it blend in with its surroundings

Carnivores animals that eat other animals

Cold-blooded an animal whose body temperature depends on its surroundings

Constrictors snakes that squeeze their prey

Hatchlings young animals that have just emerged from an egg

Herbivores animals that eat only plants

Keratin a protein found in snake scales and also in human fingernails

Species a category of related living things

Venomous animals that produce venom as a defense mechanism or to capture food

Vertebrates animals with a backbone or spine

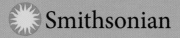

Sharks

Brenda Scott Royce

Contents

Sharks

Sharks are among the world's most fascinating creatures.

Sharks are a type of fish. Like other fish, sharks swim by moving their bodies from side to side. Sharks need to swim in order to live. They get the oxygen they need from the water around them.

? DID YOU KNOW?

More than 400 species of sharks live in the ocean. Each shark species has special features that make it unique.

At Home in the Ocean

Sharks are found in all of the world's oceans. They live in the deep dark ocean and in shallow coastal waters.

The Earth's oceans are all connected, and many sharks **migrate**, or travel long distances, in search of food or mates. Seasonal changes in water temperature are one reason sharks migrate. Blacktip sharks move south along the east coast of the United States every winter, seeking warmer waters.

Most sharks
prefer warm waters,
but Greenland sharks make
their home near the North Pole!
These huge, slow-moving sharks inhabit the icy
waters of the Arctic and North Atlantic Oceans.

Bull sharks are one of
the few shark species
that can survive in
freshwater for long
periods of time.
Bull sharks have been
known to travel long
distances up rivers,
including the Amazon,
the Mississippi, and
the Ganges.

Built to Swim

Sharks are ideally suited to a life at sea. Most have torpedo-shaped bodies that help them easily glide through water. A shark's powerful tail propels it forward. Its fins are used for steering and keeping the shark steady.

Sharks don't have bones; their skeletons are made of **cartilage**. Cartilage is lighter and more flexible than bone.

Sharks' skeletons are made of the same material as human noses and ears.

? DID YOU KNOW?

Sharks get the oxygen they need from the water around them. Depending on the species, a shark has five to seven pairs of **gills**. These slit-like openings pull oxygen from the water. Most sharks breathe by swimming with their mouths open, which allows water to pass through their gills.

great white shark's gills

Sharkskin appears smooth, but if you rub it the wrong way, it feels like sandpaper. That's because sharkskin is covered with tiny structures called **dermal denticles**. Dermal denticles are covered with enamel, just like human teeth, making sharkskin very tough.

By channeling water, dermal denticles also increase a shark's swimming speed!

Tons of Teeth

Sharks produce new teeth throughout their entire lives. If a shark loses a tooth, it gets replaced. In fact, a shark's mouth has rows of teeth waiting in line.

Some sharks lose up to 30,000 teeth in their lifetime. A great white shark has 3,000 teeth in its mouth at all times.

? DID YOU KNOW?

Venice, Florida, is known as the "shark's tooth capital of the world" due to the large number of shark teeth that wash up on its sandy beaches every year.

Sharks are often feared because of their many sharp teeth. But not all sharks have large, razorlike teeth.

Whale sharks have rows of tiny teeth. They use their teeth like a rake to sift food from the water.

The flattened back teeth of horn sharks are great for crushing the shells of clams, crabs, snails, and other prey.

All Shapes and Sizes

Sharks come in many shapes and sizes.

The gray reef shark has the familiar torpedo shape that most people associate with sharks.

The angel shark is wide and flat.

A thresher shark's enormous curved tail takes up one-third of its body weight.

The whale shark is bigger than a school bus.

The pygmy dogshark is smaller than a shoebox.

How do these sharks stack up?

whale shark: 40 feet

great white: 20 feet

hammerhead: 13 feet

tiger shark: 10 feet

zebra shark: 9 feet

shortfin mako: 7 feet

frilled shark: 6 feet

tasseled wobbegong: 5½ feet

leopard shark: 4 feet

horn shark: 3 feet

cookie-cutter shark: 20 inches

pygmy dogshark: 7 inches

? DID YOU KNOW?

In most shark species, females are larger than males.

Killer Fish

The great white shark is one of the most feared and aggressive sharks on the planet. It is an **apex predator** at the top of its **food chain**; no other animals eat it.

? DID YOU KNOW? Great white sharks have incredible senses that help them locate prey. They can detect blood from three miles away!

A great white shark eats seals, sea lions, sea turtles, and other marine animals. It has no natural enemies other than humans.

Great white sharks are found in oceans around the world. They go on long migrations to look for food.

One great white shark traveled from South Africa to Australia and back—a distance of more than 13,000 miles—in about nine months. Scientists named this long-distance swimmer "Nicole" after actor Nicole Kidman, a shark fan.

Indian Ocean

South Africa

Australia

Gentle Giant

The whale shark is the biggest fish in the world. It can weigh more than 40,000 pounds.

Despite their size, whale sharks are gentle giants rather than fierce predators. They feed mainly on plankton and small fish. Plankton are tiny organisms that drift in the ocean. The whale shark swims along with its massive mouth open and just sucks them in.

? DID YOU KNOW?

A whale shark's mouth can be five feet wide— almost large enough for a small car to drive through!

Whale sharks have polka-dotted backs. Just as no two human fingerprints are the same, each whale shark has a unique pattern of spots. Scientists use special software to help identify an individual whale shark by its markings. This software was first developed by NASA to map the stars!

Whale sharks spend most of their time alone. But they sometimes gather by the hundreds to feed. Thanks to the whale shark's peaceful nature, scientists can observe these animals up close without danger.

Looks Like...

It's easy to see how these sharks got their names.

Hammerhead

This shark's unusual head, shaped somewhat like a hammer, is used to trap stingrays by pinning them down. Stingrays are the hammerhead's favorite food. The hammerhead's eyes are at the ends of its head, allowing it to see all around, even above and below. It cannot, however, see straight ahead!

Bonnethead

The bonnethead, a member of the hammerhead family, has a rounded head. Its head is shaped like a woman's bonnet or a shovel blade (which is why bonnetheads are sometimes called shovelhead sharks).

Sawshark

This shark's snout looks like the blade of a chainsaw. The sawshark uses its saw to dig prey out of sandy sea bottoms. It will also move its head rapidly from side to side to slash at prey.

Sawsharks and sawfish look a lot alike—but only one of these animals is a shark. Sawfish are members of the ray family, along with stingrays and manta rays. The sawshark's barbels—a pair of whiskerlike protrusions on the snout—are one way to tell them apart.

sawfish

Spots and Stripes

Tiger Shark)))))

The vertical stripes on young tiger sharks give this species its name. When the shark grows up, its stripes will fade or disappear. These aggressive sharks have sharp, curved teeth, which allow them to rip through the shells of sea turtles. They also eat other sharks, seabirds, and sea mammals.

Zebra Shark)))))

The zebra shark has stripes like a zebra when it is born. Like the tiger shark, the zebra shark loses its stripes when it reaches adulthood. Adult zebra sharks have spots instead of stripes.

baby zebra shark

Leopard Shark :•:•:

Like a leopard found in a forest, the leopard shark is covered in spots. Because their mouths are located on the undersides of their heads, they can eat crabs, clams, and fish eggs that they find on the ocean floor. The leopard shark's spots serve as camouflage, helping it blend in with its surroundings.

adult zebra shark

Weird and Wonderful

One of the strangest shark species on the planet, the cookie-cutter shark gets its name from its odd style of eating. It bites with its pointy lower teeth and then spins its body around, slicing a circular chunk of flesh off its prey.

? DID YOU KNOW?

These small sharks have been known to attack animals much larger than themselves—including great white sharks!

With fringes that resemble seaweed, the tasseled wobbegong is a master of disguise. This odd-looking bottom-dweller

blends right in with coral reefs and algae-covered rocks. When a fish swims within reach, the wobbegong opens its large mouth and sucks it in.

The bramble shark has thorny scales covering its body.

Can a shark glow in the dark? Tiny organs called photophores on the lantern shark's skin produce light.

The epaulette shark can swim, but it mainly moves by "walking" on the ocean bottom, using its fins as legs!

Shark Records

BIGGEST:

At more than 40 feet long, the whale shark easily wins the prize for the biggest fish in the sea.

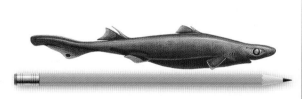

At about six inches in length, the dwarf lantern shark is most likely the world's smallest shark.

fastest:

The shortfin mako holds the record for fastest swimming speed by a shark. One mako was clocked at more than 40 miles per hour.

strongest bite:

Bull sharks have the greatest bite strength of any shark, even beating out the great white!

deadliest diet:

Hammerhead sharks may have the most dangerous eating habits of any shark. Stingrays, their favorite food, have sharp venomous spines on their tails. One hammerhead was found with nearly a hundred stingray spines in its mouth!

deepest diver:

The Portuguese dogfish has been found at depths of nearly 10,000 feet.

Shark Ancestors

Sharks have been around for approximately 400 million years. That's 200 million years before dinosaurs roamed the Earth!

While some types of sharks have survived for millions of years, others have gone **extinct**.

The largest shark that ever lived was Megalodon. This prehistoric predator may have reached 60 feet in length.

Scientists can tell a lot about Megalodon from **fossil** evidence. Fossilized Megalodon teeth measuring up to seven inches in length have been found.

fossilized Megalodon shark tooth and great white shark tooth

male Falcatus fossil

Falcatus was a foot-long shark that lived over 300 million years ago. Males had a forward-facing spine protruding from their backs. Females did not have this spine. Numerous Falcatus fossils have been found in Montana, which was once beneath the sea.

DID YOU KNOW? The oldest complete shark fossil found to date is over 400 million years old. The ancient specimen of *Doliodus problematicus*, a small shark measuring less than a foot in length, was found in New Brunswick, Canada.

shark fossil

Studying Sharks

Biologists have been using ROVs (remotely operated vehicles) for decades to get a better look at undersea life. ROVs can travel into waters that are too deep or dangerous for a human diver. In 2012, biologists using an ROV discovered a previously unknown shark species, the Galapagos catshark.

Despite using the latest technology to study sharks, there is still a lot to learn about these fascinating fish.

GPS (Global Positioning System) technology uses satellites to pinpoint locations anywhere on Earth. Many cars are equipped with GPS devices, which help direct drivers to their destinations. Biologists are now using GPS on sharks!

A device containing a tiny transmitter is attached to the shark, allowing the shark's movements to be tracked. The data collected by these and other types of satellite tags help biologists learn more about shark behavior and migration patterns.

? DID YOU KNOW? You can go online to track the travel routes of tagged sharks. Some sharks even have their own Twitter accounts!

Threats to Sharks

Sharks play an important role in keeping our oceans healthy. When the top animal in a food chain disappears, its absence causes problems down the chain. If great white sharks were removed from an area, the number of seals (a favorite food item) would greatly increase. Too many hungry seals means not enough fish to go around. Eventually, the entire **ecosystem** would collapse.

What is the greatest threat to sharks? Humans. It is estimated that around 100 million sharks are killed by humans each year.

Overfishing is the major cause of shark deaths each year. Because sharks grow slowly and only produce several young during their lifetime, more sharks are killed before they can grow their numbers.

One major cause of shark deaths is shark fin soup. Shark fin soup is a delicacy in parts of Asia. Fishermen catch sharks, cut off their fins, and throw their bodies back in the ocean. This is called finning.

To protect sharks from the practice of finning, the U.S. Congress passed the Shark Conservation Act in 2010. Several countries have banned shark fishing altogether.

Sharks Quiz

1. Sharks are what type of animal?
   a. Mammal
   b. Fish
   c. Whale
   d. Amphibian

2. What shark can survive in freshwater for long periods of time?
   a. Tiger shark
   b. Great white shark
   c. Bull shark
   d. Thresher shark

3. What causes sharkskin to feel like sandpaper?
   a. Dermal denticles
   b. Barnacles
   c. Algae
   d. Hair

4. About how many teeth does a great white shark have in its mouth at all times?
   a. 3,000
   b. 150
   c. 88
   d. 1,237

5. Which is the largest shark?
   a. Pygmy dogshark
   b. Tiger Shark
   c. Whale shark
   d. Thresher shark

6. Which shark has an unusual head that is used to pin down prey?
   a. Zebra shark
   b. Hammerhead shark
   c. Leopard shark
   d. Bramble shark

7. What are photophores?
   a. Tiny organisms that drift in the ocean
   b. Spots on leopard sharks
   c. Tiny organs that produce light
   d. Remotely operated vehicles

8. What is the greatest threat to sharks?
   a. Whales
   b. Stingrays
   c. Sea lions
   d. Humans

Glossary

apex predator an animal at the top of its food chain; no animals eat it

biologists people who study plants or animals

cartilage light, flexible material from which a shark's skeleton is made

dermal denticles tiny toothlike structures covering a shark's skin

ecosystem a community of all the living things in an area

extinct a species that no longer exists

food chain the order that animals eat plants and other animals

fossil a trace or print or the remains of a plant or animal preserved in soil or rock

gills organs used by fish that allow them to breathe underwater

migrate to move across long distances

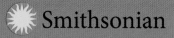
Big Cats and Other Predators

Brenda Scott Royce

Contents

What Is a Predator?

Predators inspire fear and fascination. We tend to think of them as bloodthirsty beasts, but not all predators are large, aggressive animals.

A predator is any animal that hunts another animal for food. Predators range in size and may be **solitary** or social, speedy or slow-moving.

Predators are born with hunting skills according to their environment and their **prey**. All predators must kill in order to survive.

Food Chain

Predators are a natural and necessary part of every food chain. A food chain is a series of living things in which the next lower member is used as a source of food.

A food chain starts with plants, which get their energy from sunlight. Herbivores get energy from eating the plants. Carnivores get their energy from eating other animals. Omnivores eat both plants and animals for energy.

Healthy ecosystems depend on balanced food chains. If one animal's food source disappears, the other animals in the food chain will be affected.

Some animals are both predator *and* prey. While these animals are hunting for food, they must also be on the lookout for larger animals seeking to attack them.

Armadillos are predators that feed on ants and termites. Wild cats and birds prey upon armadillos. The three-banded armadillo's thick shell and its ability to curl into a tight ball protect it from most enemies, but a jaguar's powerful jaws can pierce through this armor.

? Did You Know?

In a healthy ecosystem, prey will always outnumber predators.

Life at the Top

An animal at the top of its food chain is called an **apex predator**. Once fully grown, these animals have no natural enemies other than humans. African lions, killer whales, and saltwater crocodiles are examples of apex predators.

Polar bears are the top predators of the Arctic region. They hunt for seals and other marine mammals by waiting near breathing holes in the ice.

The Bengal tiger hunts a wide variety of prey. No other animal hunts the tiger.

The gray wolf is top dog in any ecosystem it inhabits. Where their habitat overlaps with coyotes or cougars, gray wolves outcompete these rivals for food.

fossa

Madagascar's top predator—the fossa—faces no competition from lions or cheetahs. The fossa has retractable claws that can come out like a cat's claws. These claws help the fossa as it climbs swiftly through trees in pursuit of lemurs.

lemur

Built to Kill

Predators are born with features that enable them to hunt. Some are equipped with fangs or stingers for delivering a deadly dose of **venom**. Some predators have sharp teeth or beaks, while others have claws that slash and stab.

Lions have retractable claws that extend like switchblades when it's time to attack. A lion's tongue is rough like sandpaper, which helps the cat rip apart meat.

Scorpions have a stinger at the tip of their tail to inject venom into their prey.

A grizzly bear uses its sharp claws to fish for salmon.

Super long and lightning fast, the chameleon's tongue is a marvelous tool for catching insects! It has a sticky tip that forms a small suction cup when it strikes its target.

The boa constrictor uses its entire body as a weapon, wrapping around its prey and slowly squeezing the air from its lungs.

Super Skills

Sharp senses help predators detect prey. Speed and agility come in handy when chasing or stalking. Strength is a major asset in making the kill.

The cheetah—the fastest land mammal—can chase down prey at speeds of up to 70 miles per hour.

Owls have keen eyesight and great hearing—traits that make them excellent hunters.

Sharks have the same five senses humans have (sight, smell, hearing, taste, and touch), but they also have a sixth sense. Sharks can detect the electrical impulses given off by other animals in the water. This helps sharks locate fish hiding nearby.

Prey are born with skills that help them avoid being hunted and killed. Some are fast runners, and some zigzag when they run. Some have coloring that act as **camouflage** and helps them hide. Some simply taste bad or are poisonous to eat.

How They Hunt

Predators have different ways of capturing prey. The alligator snapping turtle tricks its prey, using its own tongue as bait! Sitting with its mouth wide open, the turtle flails its pink tongue around like a worm, hoping to lure a hungry fish.

Ambush predators are masters of surprise. Rather than chasing their prey, they hide and wait for prey to come to them.

The praying mantis blends in with leaves. When it spots its prey, the mantis springs into action, grasping the victim with its spiked legs and eating it alive.

Some animals team up to take down prey. Hunting in a group is generally more successful than hunting alone.

Killer whales, or orcas, usually hunt in family groups, called pods, of up to 40 other orcas. Members of a pod work together to surround a school of fish, and then they slap their strong tails against their prey. This stuns the fish, which the orcas then eat.

Overachievers

Most predators are content to pick on prey smaller than themselves. But some have their eyes on a bigger prize.

Mountain lions are solitary hunters. Killing large mammals, like deer and elk, requires strength and skill. A mountain lion usually bites the back of the neck of its prey.

Thanks to extremely flexible jaws and an expanding throat, the egg-eating snake can swallow an egg much larger than its own head.

Komodo dragons can kill prey as large as water buffalo! Water buffalo often manage to escape the initial attack, but shock and blood loss— perhaps quickened by venom in the dragon's bite—prove overwhelming.

Officially declared the world's most venomous spider, Brazilian wandering spiders often eat frogs, mice, lizards, and birds.

Aerial Predators

Birds of prey—also known as raptors—share many characteristics that make them great hunters: forward-facing eyes, sharp talons (claws), and hooked beaks. This group of animals includes eagles, hawks, falcons, and owls.

Birds of prey usually attack from behind to minimize the chance of being seen until it is too late.

Harpy eagles' talons are bigger than a grizzly bear's claws! Harpy eagles can snatch monkeys and sloths right out of the treetops.

Osprey are also known as "fish hawks" because of their skill at catching live fish. These large birds often hover briefly over the water before diving—feet first—to grab a fish.

Not all predatory birds are classified as raptors. Kingfishers are great at catching fish—but they also eat frogs and lizards, snatching them up in their long, thick bills.

Herons can stand completely still in shallow water for more than an hour waiting for prey (mostly fish and frogs) to come within reach.

Marine Predators

Although commonly called "killer whales," orcas are actually the largest member of the dolphin family. They use their 4-inch-long teeth to slice through their prey.

When piranhas close their mouths, the triangular teeth fit together like a zipper! These fish rarely waste energy attacking healthy prey, preferring to go after weak and injured creatures.

One of the deadliest predators in the ocean could fit in the palm of your hand! The blue-ringed octopus is about the size of a golf ball, but its venom is thousands of times stronger than cyanide, which can kill humans in only minutes.

The great white shark is the largest predatory fish. These sharks can swim up to 35 miles per hour, and have up to 300 teeth in their mouth at one time. Large marine mammals are no match for these toothy terrors.

Emperor penguins dive deep to catch fish. The penguin has barbs on its tongue to prevent slippery fish from escaping.

Desert Predators

Desert dwellers have to be resourceful. Only the toughest animals can survive in areas where food and water are hard to come by.

Coyotes are omnivores, and adjust their hunting style depending on what food is available. They will team up to hunt deer, but for smaller prey they prefer going solo.

Rattlesnakes have folding fangs that swing into striking position when they open their mouth wide. Most rattlers strike quickly and then release their victim. They wait nearby for the venom to take effect.

? Did You Know?

When threatened, rattlesnakes hiss and rattle their tails to frighten intruders. When hunting, they use a silent approach instead of the rattle.

Roadrunners seldom fly. They seize scorpions by the tail and don't shy away from attacking snakes. They typically batter their prey, smashing it against the ground or a rock.

Like many desert animals, the shrew can survive without drinking water. It gets the moisture it needs from its prey.

The desert tarantula has two large fangs for injecting venom. The venom turns its prey's insides into a soupy mush.

Jungle Predators

Found mainly in Central and South America, jaguars prefer large prey. They are good climbers and will often ambush their prey by leaping down from trees.

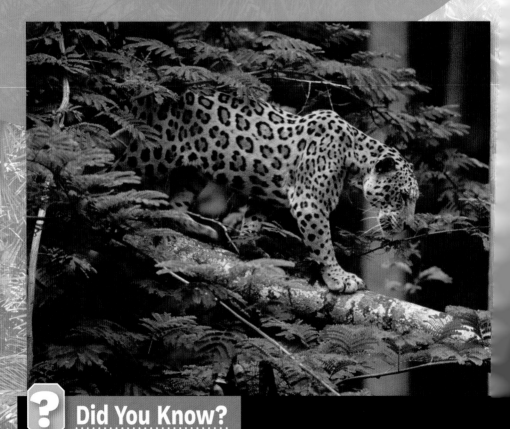

? Did You Know?

The name *jaguar* comes from a Native American word that means "beast who kills with one leap."

The tree frog's color helps it blend in with tree leaves. It hides on a leaf waiting for insects to approach, then snatches them with a quick flick of its sticky tongue.

At up to 550 pounds, the anaconda is the world's largest snake. This massive serpent makes its home in the South American tropics. Anacondas constrict their prey, squeezing until the animal can't breathe. Loosely hinged jaws allow anacondas to swallow their prey whole—no matter the size.

Predator Plants

There are more than 720 carnivorous plant species on the planet. Most live in areas where there are few nutrients in the soil. Most get their energy by consuming insects. These predators wait for prey to wander into their trap.

The Venus flytrap is probably the most famous of the predatory plants. When an insect touches the tiny "trigger hairs" on a flytrap's leaf, its two halves quickly snap shut—trapping whatever is inside.

Insects attracted to the glistening leaves of the butterwort are in for a sticky surprise! The plant's leaves are coated in a greasy liquid that traps bugs.

? Did You Know?

Carnivorous plants have been known to consume frogs, lizards, small rodents, fish, and—in rare cases—birds.

Picky Eaters

Specialist predators eat only one type of prey. The snail kite (a type of hawk) dines only on snails. Australia's fat-tailed gecko is a termite specialist, and will often go hungry rather than settle for a different bug. **Opportunistic predators** will eat nearly any animal they can catch.

Blue whales have one thing on their minds at suppertime—krill! These huge whales take in great mouthfuls of water and strain it through their jaw. Thousands of krill are left behind for the whale to eat.

Black-footed ferrets eat prairie dogs—and almost nothing else. When prairie dog colonies began to disappear, the black-footed ferret was in trouble! In 1986, there were fewer than 20 black-footed ferrets left on the planet. Conservation efforts have helped increase their numbers, but they are still **endangered**.

Survival Lessons

How do predators acquire these amazing hunting abilities? Many young predators learn through play. Play provides practice for real situations, allowing young animals to challenge themselves.

During play fights, animals are careful not to hurt one another. Play sessions for tiger cubs help them gain strength and speed.

Wolf pups learn to handle competition by play-fighting. Play helps wolves establish bonds of friendship, which are important for pack animals.

Another way animals learn is through observation. Sea otters learn their hunting skills by watching the actions of role models. In addition to learning *how* to hunt, young predators must learn which animals make good prey.

Cheetah mothers often release injured prey to give their cubs the opportunity to make the kill. The prey animal may escape from the inexperienced cub, but improving the cub's hunting skills—and increasing its odds of survival—are worth the risk.

VIPs: Very Important Predators

Predators play a vital role in keeping ecosystems healthy. The disappearance of a predator can lead to disastrous changes for the animals that share its habitat.

Bald eagles and island foxes lived together on California's Channel Islands for years. The bald eagles, which mostly preyed on fish and were not interested in eating the foxes, began disappearing from the islands in the 1960s, mainly due to **pesticide** poisoning.

Without bald eagles on the island, the golden eagle, a new predator that did prey on foxes, moved in. In less than 10 years, golden eagles killed 95 percent of the foxes!

Today, biologists are working to restore the natural balance on the Channel Islands, making them once again safe for the island fox.

People are predators, too. We eat both plant and animal foods. We are at the top of many food chains.

Many predators need our protection. Snow leopards live in the mountains of central Asia, where they are an apex predator. Threats to the snow leopard include habitat loss, illegal hunting, and reduction of available prey. They are currently classified as endangered.

People often take pity on prey animals and view predators as "bad guys." But to keep our ecosystems healthy and balanced, we need them both.

Predators Quiz

1. **What is a predator?**
   a. Any animal eaten by another animal
   b. Any mammal that eats animals
   c. Any animal that hunts another animal for food
   d. Any large, aggressive animal

2. **Who gets their energy from eating only plants?**
   a. Carnivore
   b. Herbivore
   c. Predator
   d. Omnivore

3. **What is the top predator in Madagascar?**
   a. The Bengal tiger
   b. The lemur
   c. The cheetah
   d. The fossa

4. **What is an ambush predator?**
   a. A predator that waits for prey to come to ther
   b. A predator that chases prey
   c. A predator that hunts in groups
   d. A predator that swims

5. **Which does NOT kill prey larger than itself?**
   a. Mountain lion
   b. Orca
   c. Komodo dragon
   d. Brazilian wandering spider

6. **Which is NOT a raptor?**
   a. Eagle
   b. Owl
   c. Kingfisher
   d. Hawk

7. **What animal family do killer whales belong to?**
   a. Orca family
   b. Fish family
   c. Shark family
   d. Dolphin family

8. **What animal's name means "beast who kills with one leap"?**
   a. Jaguar
   b. Hyena
   c. Fossa
   d. Leopard

Answers: 1) c 2) b 3) d 4) a 5) b 6) c 7) d 8) a

Glossary

ambush predators predators that hide and wait for prey

apex predator an animal at the top of its food chain

camouflage an animal's colors or markings that allow it to blend in with its surroundings

endangered at risk of becoming extinct

opportunistic predators predators that will eat whatever food is available

pesticide a poison used to kill pests such as insect

prey an animal that is hunted and killed by another animal for food

solitary alone

specialist predators predators that eat only one type of prey

venom a chemical produced by animals such as snakes, spiders, and scorpions and usually injecte by biting or stinging